Creative Hands
Carol Tompkins-Parker

Readers are encouraged to go to www.MissionPointPress.com to contact the author or to find information on how to buy this book in bulk at a discounted rate.

Published by Mission Point Press
2554 Chandler Rd.
Traverse City, MI 49696
(231) 421-9513

www.MissionPointPress.com

Cover: "Creative Hands" by Carol Tompkins-Parker
Artist drawing the artist's own hands

ISBN: 978-1-943995-23-3
Library of Congress Control Number: 2021901433

Printed in the United States of America

This book is dedicated to the influential men in my life:

To my husband Edward Parker, the love of my life;
To my father Richard Tompkins, my hero;
To Frederick G. Attebury, my favourite art education professor and mentor; and
To John Robert Williams, my dear friend and photographer for this book.

Foreword

Our hands.

Eight fingers, two opposable thumbs and flexibility at the wrist. A part of our body used the most daily, without thought. Ten digits taken for granted.

Until something goes horribly wrong.

As an artist, I use my hands for creating intricate etchings and drawings, currently compiling a series of other people's hands depicting a wide variety of activities. The drawings illustrate the skills each person is known to possess. The irony of needing hand surgery whilst trying to complete this unique and demanding project is not lost on me. But, it is nearly impossible for me to hold a pencil for hours and draw, to the perfection that I demand of myself and my finished artwork.

Nearly all my life has meant enduring chronic pain, finally being diagnosed with juvenile rheumatoid arthritis and systemic lupus erythematosus on February 14, 1974, at the age of 18, by Dr. James Cassidy, head of the Rheumatology Department, University of Michigan Hospital in Ann Arbor, Michigan. For almost a decade prior, I had struggled with poor health, plus persistent pain and swollen joints throughout my frail, skinny body. At an early age, I came to accept my being so accident prone, truly a total klutz. I correlated the continual pain, overall weakness, and the inability to participate in daily activities to my fullest capacity with profound frustration. But, I refused then, as now, to allow pain and poor balance to dictate nor define my life.

The most painful joints have been my hands, wrists and knees. In and out of local hospitals, plus the University of Michigan Hospital, oftentimes for months, treated by a myriad of specialists, testing and over three dozen surgeries have become the norm of my life.

In the mid-1980s, orthopedic surgeon Dr. Mark Leslie of Traverse City, Michigan, performed my first tendon surgery on both hands, first on my right, then a couple months later on the left. These were followed by silicone joint replacements at the major metacarpal joint, again the right hand followed almost two years later on the left.

Approximately four years after joint replacement, my right wrist was fused with a titanium plate and seven titanium screws. One screw dislodged and was surgically removed; I can actually say I have a screw loose! Five years later, the left wrist was partially fused, minus hardware.

The expected livelihood of these silicone "joints" are 15 years, due to the wear-and-tear our hands are subjected to daily. My joints have been protected for 30-plus years with thick keloid scarring, both helpful and a hindrance. The scarring limits my fingers' mobility and dexterity.

Double the lifespan of the silicone implanted joints, and all four have sadly and collectively deteriorated and broken in my right hand.

First, the ring finger on my dominant hand broke, a visible space between my knuckles and finger bone shown on the X-ray. As the ring and little finger share ligaments moving in tandem, both developed severe ulnar deviation. In layman's terms, now bending at a 45-degree angle away from the other fingers, towards the ulna, or outer bone from wrist to elbow.

Next, the middle finger became another overly flexible joint, also broken, suddenly accompanying the ring and pinkie fingers in tandem deviation. I am unable to bring these fingers towards my index finger, which now stands alone, a perpetual "peace" or "V for victory" sign. I am quite a contortionist with my fingers!

The broken joints themselves do not hurt, but the fast and drastic crippling of my fingers is causing frustrating, continuous pain. It travels from fingers to wrist to elbow, terminating at my shoulder, making sleep insufferable, and performing most anything difficult. My grasp is limited to the thumb and index finger. Enough to provide a "death grip" on a bike handle whilst riding our tandem bicycle with my husband, Edward.

Tomorrow, I see Mark for my first surgery consultation in about four years. The remembrance of the excruciating post-op pain, the nausea, fingers swollen like sausages, bound in protective compression post-op wrapping the size of a small football, throbbing pain with every heartbeat, and the months of torturous physical therapy memories loom. Due to my compromised immune system with lupus and several other autoimmune diseases, I am highly susceptible to infections. Complications and infection I fear more than the surgery.

I truly can look at my hands in wonderment, knowing how deformed they were before Dr. Leslie started correcting these precious appendages over three decades. I cry silently and frequently, seeing how quickly my right hand became crippled and nearly useless, returning back to the disfigurement last seen in the mid-1980s.

I have reverted to deliberately hiding my hand, as years previous, extremely self-conscious of its appearance. Soon, I can rejoice in gaining the use and visible correction of this physical setback.

Happy dance forthcoming in the near future!

As I have learned to live with chronic illnesses, mysterious ailments, testing and surgeries, friends and family refer to me as brave, strong, an inspiration and a hero. I blush at the descriptors. I do not consider myself a hero nor brave, never seeking sympathy for my life's situation. My goal is to live life by example, to enjoy every moment to its fullest, with determination, persistence and stubbornness, whilst an advocate in awareness of arthritis, lupus and other autoimmune diseases. There is no other way I know how to live my life, it's just who I am.

This surgery joint replacement surgery is just another speed bump and minor obstacle in my life. Untimely and out of my control, it will soon be resolved.

As I frequently say, "it could be worse...."

Postscript

My joint replacement reconstruction surgery took place on February 22, 2019, with no post-operative complications and surprisingly, very little pain. All of the titanium screws and plate were removed, which I have kept. Physical therapy for my "new" hand continued into late October 2019.

Two pairs of the removed titanium screws were made into earrings, drilled into animal bone. I love doing the unexpected!

Sadly, in late May 2019, I severely injured the ligaments in my left "good" hand, whilst raking and shoveling. This injury required emergency surgery on May 30th. My lengthy physical therapy with hand therapists Maritza Sheehan and Kate Holtfretter, plus Virginia Willette-Green unexpectedly involved both hands. Recuperation and regaining the full use of both hands has been frustratingly slower than I anticipated. I am not a patient person.

But, I am on the mend....

This drawing project began as a notecards donation to the Rumple Quilt Kins quilt show a decade ago. Every member was asked to contribute ten items to sell at the guild fundraising booth.

Most members would bring quilting accessories or pre-cut material. My husband Edward suggested I offer a drawing. "How many of them can draw?" he asked me.

I delivered ten sets of notecards, each with six cards and envelopes featuring my arthritic hands quilting. Nine sets were sold. The hand series was born!

The popularity of those first notecard sales at several art fairs reinforced my pursuit of drawing other people depicting activities for which they are known.

The process of contacting fellow creative people that I know, explaining my proposition and allowing me to photograph and draw their hands has been a long, frustrating but productive process.

I am too stubborn to allow my arthritic, deformed hands prevent my detailed drawings and every day life.

CAROL TOMPKINS-PARKER
"CAROL QUILTING"

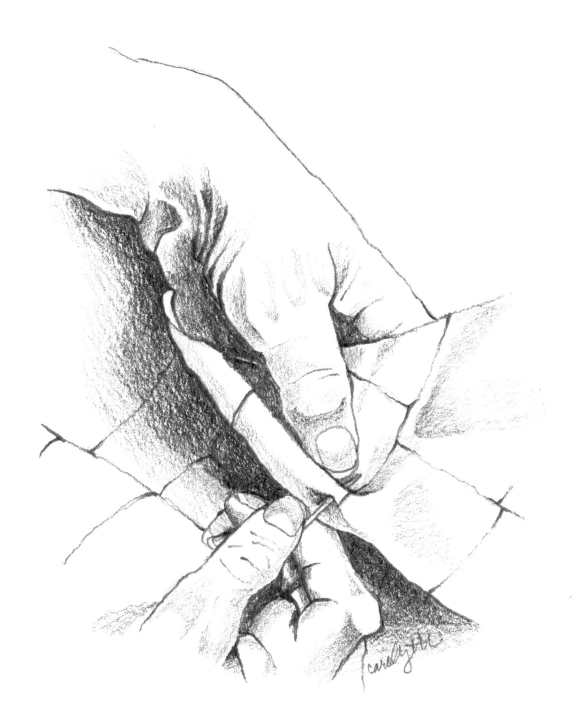

We met at the inaugural Sleeping Bear Mountain Bike Classic race that Edward Parker co-founded with the bike shops from Traverse City, MI. I was pulled from the crowd of spectators to volunteer at the event. The Homestead Resort of Glen Arbor, MI, hosted the races the first several years.

At the fourth annual race in 1989, the event relocated that year to Sugar Loaf Resort near Cedar, MI, Edward managed for us to work together. We started dating a month later and have been together since early October 1989.

We were married in June 1994 at Otter Creek beach on the shores of Lake Michigan, near Empire, MI. The shoreline is a small portion of the Sleeping Bear Dunes National Lakeshore, extending into Benzie and Leelanau Counties in Northwest Michigan.

He was the mechanic at The Sports Shop of Beulah until its owner retired, plus manager/mechanic of Weiler Cycle Works, also in Beulah, MI. He can fix, construct or custom paint any bike. Edward has a small bike shop filled with a wide array of professional bike-specific tools and equipment. He possesses bikes upstairs and downstairs in our house, plus other buildings.

An outdoorsman and avid cyclist, he is one of the founding members of the Cherry Capital Cycling Club. He volunteers as mechanic each spring at the Recycle-A-Bicycle sale and swap, plus contributing his repair skills with Norte, a bike centric advocacy youth program.

Yes, Edward is a bike junkie, "the bike guy", local repair guru, a Mr. Fix-It, and a former chef. He is currently a driver in public transportation with the regional Bay Area Transportation Authority.

He is also the funniest, kindest, most generous and loving man I know, who serenades me every morning, off-key but gleefully. Edward has been at my side as we have endured the good and bad, is very supportive and protective as my health has declined over the years. He is my hero, best friend, and I cannot imagine life without him.

Ever thine,

Ever mine,

Ever ours.

EDWARD PARKER
"EDWARD CYCLING"

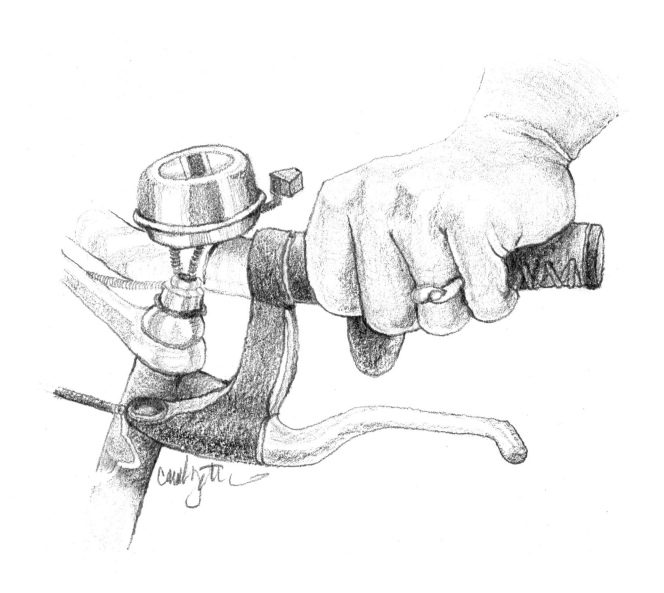

My father, Richard Tompkins, was a man of many talents. But foremost he was a wonderful, generous and loving father.

He proudly served in the US Army Air Corps, stationed at Swindon, England, where I was born, northwest of London, during the Korean War. He was a Traverse City firefighter and state fire inspector for 25 years. He was instrumental in starting the emergency services at the fire department in the late 1960s.

Dad taught us outdoor skills such as camping, canoeing, fishing and skiing. As a family, we enjoyed many vacations, and made several cross country trips. He insisted we all know first aid, CPR and the Heinrich maneuvre. Between work and teaching first aid, he was also a dedicated Cub Scout and Boy Scout leader.

He could fix almost anything, told bad puns, introduced me to Monty Python and had a great sense humour. My bizarre sense of humour, pale blue eyes and curly hair I attribute to Dad.

My hero and rock died on June 11, 2011, the day Edward and I celebrated our 17th wedding anniversary.

I miss you so much every day, Dad.

RICHARD TOMPKINS
"TURN THE PAGE"

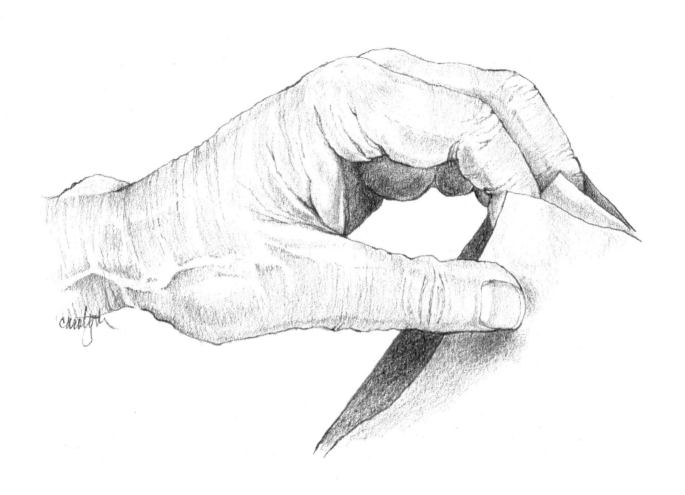

A talented Master Gardener, school teaching aide and gentle woman, Laura Kirby is the most grounded and environmentally conscious person I know.

We met decades ago, part of a like-minded group of friends, plus we were members of the Bayside Travellers country dance group.

A devoted wife and mother, for at least a decade Laura continues as a 4H leader for dozens of kids in Leelanau County.

Whenever Edward and I are challenged and truly perplexed with a gardening issue, she is our "go-to" person and plant lifesaver.

As my hands project expanded, I knew only one person's hands that could depict a garden specialist, hands down. (Pun intended!)

She, three or four other women and myself would have a "gals' weekend" usually in the Upper Peninsula of Michigan. I miss those silly times together, something I hope we can resume.

Thank you for your generosity, knowledge, love and years of friendship, Laura.

LAURA KIRBY
"PRUNING SHEARS"

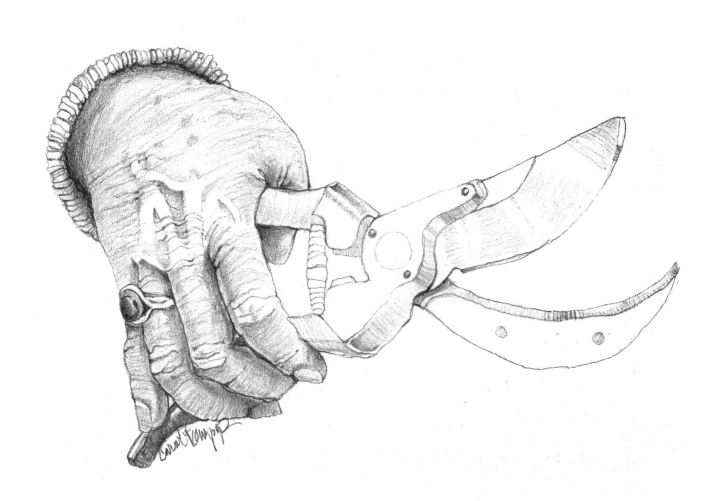

I first met Nancy Crow at a monthly meeting of the Rumple Quilt Kins quilt guild in the village of Interlochen, MI, in the early 2000s.
I returned to the guild a few years ago, having moved back to Traverse City from Las Vegas, New Mexico.

Retired from business, Nancy "took up" quilting, taking a couple classes, attending guild weekend workshops and is an accomplished quilter.

Living a short distance from each other, we frequently carpooled to the guild meetings. Time spent travelling together gave us an additional opportunity to discuss the "show-and-tell" finished quilted pieces exhibited that night, techniques or new block patterns.

Guild members are always working on multiple projects and different mediums. A skilled knitter, Nancy is always busy with handwork at the small weekly guild members' gathering.

NANCY CROW
"NANCY KNITTING"

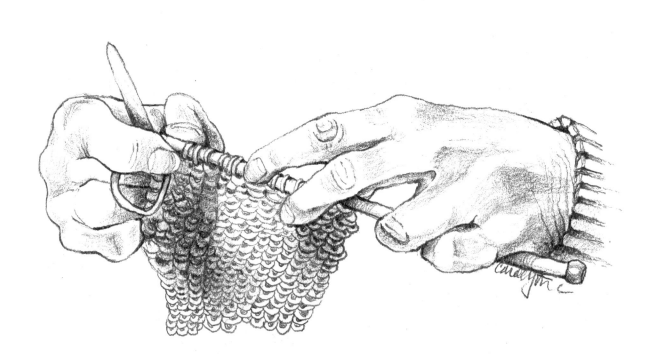

My dear friend Tonja Carlson and I met in college, residing on the same floor in the women's dorm at Northwestern Michigan College in Traverse City, MI. We made money that summer sewing patches on the uniforms of cadets in the Great Lakes Maritime Academy.

Whilst in high school, Tonja was shown beading in the early 1970s by a Choctaw Native American at Fort Michilimackinac in Mackinaw City, MI. Early and Native American histories influence her beading and jewellery making.

"Beading is habit forming and calorie free", she likes to say, with a smile.

Thank you for offering your shoulders to lean upon during some scary or sorrowful times, your encouragement and sharing your husband's bad puns. Love you for decades, Tonja, for memories and fun times past, knowing more adventures and memories are yet to come.

TONJA CARLSON
"JEWELRY MAKING"

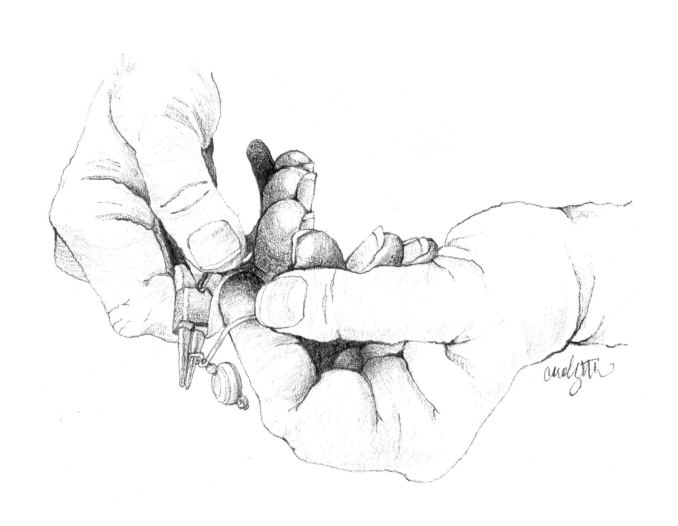

Chris and I have known each other since childhood, as our family lived next door to the Bazzetts from the late 1960s to mid-1980s. I feel like the adopted "fifth" daughter of their family.

A devoted mother, grandmother, plus a day care provider, my dear friend possesses the most calming and generous presence of all of my friends. Chris is a friend whom I can stop by unannounced but welcomed with genuine love and always a big hug. Many times I have cried on her shoulder, seeking advice and reassurance.

For 30 years, she and her late husband Ben Hansen, hosted an annual Christmas Day open house. We miss that all-day event and comradery.

I drew her hand holding a Christmas tree bulb, in honour of her 30 years graciously opening her home and heart to us.

I love you, dear Chris!

CHRIS BAZZETT
"CHRIS AT CHRISTMAS"

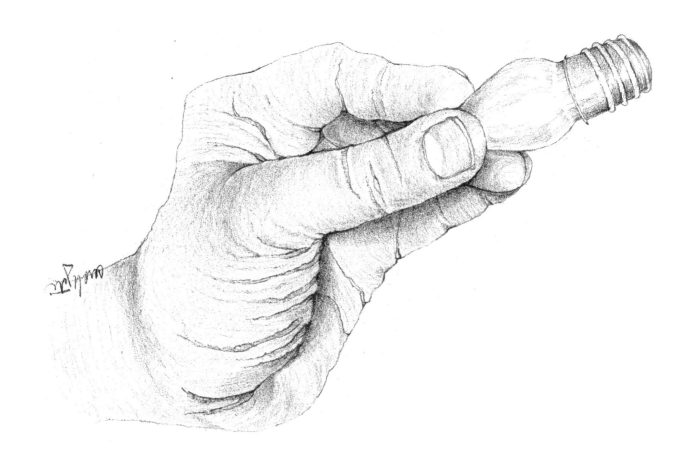

Connie Stevens is another member of the Rumple Quilt Kins guild, which meets monthly at the old library in the village of Interlochen, MI.

With her shears, she is shown cutting small pieces of material for a hand appliqué quilt. Connie has shared numerous hand and machine wall hangings and quilts at the monthly meetings.

A quilter for decades, Connie is another guild member who I admire with her creativity in her many quilts and appliqué pieces. She has graciously shared and exhibited her work for years, either at the weekly handwork gathering or the monthly guild meetings.

Thank you, Connie.

CONNIE STEVENS
"CONNIE CUTTING"

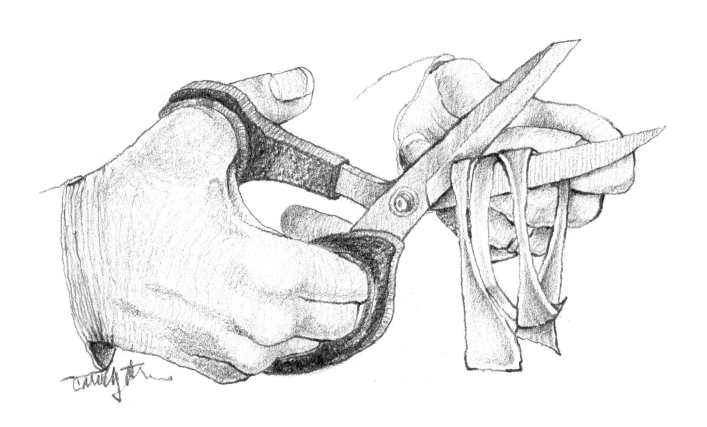

Barb Deroshia-Stacks and I met years ago at Rebecca's Studio, an artist co-op studio in the Warehouse district. Jewellery and lamp work (hand blown glass) were the predominant art vendors at the studio. It was the first business where I started selling my hand drawing notecards.

A talented jeweller, Barb works in sterling silver with native Michigan Petoskey stones.
Her interests in the arts she attributes to long walks on Lake Michigan with her dad, identifying fossils.

Barb took classes in metal smithing, stone cutting, polishing and shaping at Northwestern Michigan College in Traverse City, MI.
Her education continues in new techniques, styles and mixed mediums.

I long wished I had the hand strength to make the gorgeous one-of-a-kind pieces that Barb creates.

BARB DEROSHIA-STACKS
"SILVER WORK"

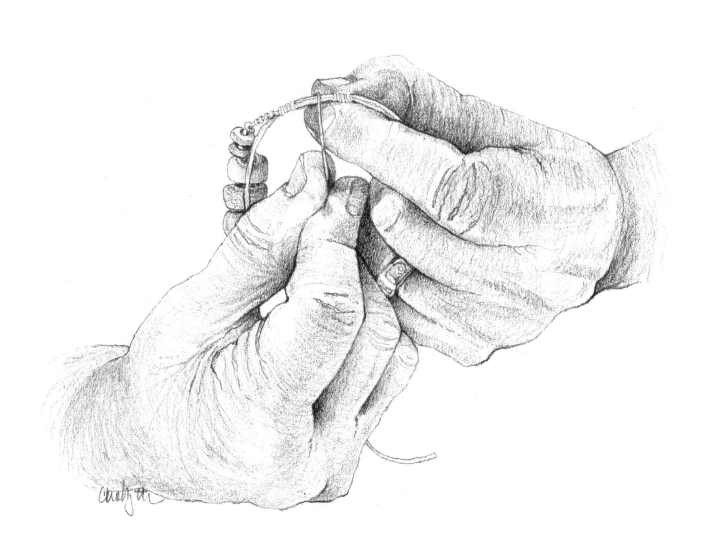

Josh is my husband Edward's eldest son. With his wife Amber, they are parents of son Alex, and daughter Ella, a very sports-minded family.

A Kingsley, MI, high school coach in softball and former assistant football coach, Josh is very involved with their village school and sports programs. Alex is attending Central Michigan University in Mount Pleasant, MI on a baseball scholarship, whilst Ella is on the Kingsley High School Girls Softball team.

As Josh and then four-year-old Ella were walking hand-in-hand to their family van years ago, I took a quick photo of their intertwined hands. This drawing is the most popular print and notecard that people purchase.

I am so proud of all of you.

JOSH PARKER AND DAUGHTER ELLA
"FATHER AND CHILD"

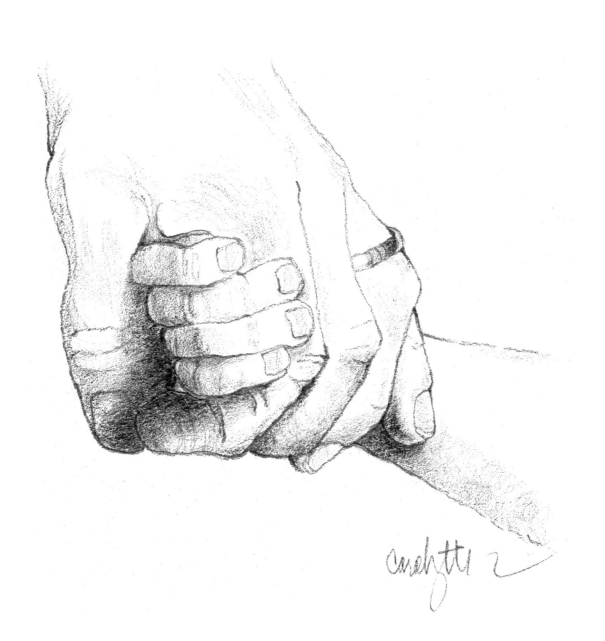

I met Jackie Baase at a cross country ski party she and her husband Steve hosted in February 1990. At that gathering of their family and friends, I had no idea the impact and friendship that would develop.

Her husband is one of my husband Edward's best friends since childhood. The two men and Jackie had been friends for decades. Dating and marrying Edward, I made it a quartet. Steve was best man and Jackie co-matron of honour at our wedding on the shores of Lake Michigan.

Jackie has an Associate degree in the medical program from Northwestern Michigan College in Traverse City, MI. For 35 years she was the office manager at the Michigan State University Northwest Michigan Horticultural Research Station in Leelanau County.

Upon retirement, she and Steve owned The Art of Framing and Gallery in Traverse City for five years. We have helped each other's household move and offered other help over the years.

Thank you Jackie, for your years of friendship and support.

JACKIE BAASE
"PAINTING"

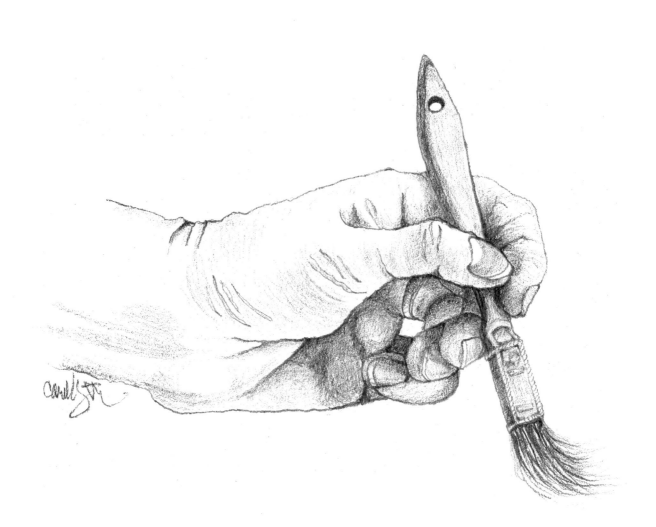

My husband Edward and I met Tim Burke and his family decades ago. As fellow residents of Benzie County, our paths crossed frequently at various events.

It was a thrill to work with him at Interlochen Public Radio for almost two years. He was one of the on-air personalities, broadcasting diverse genres of music, playing folk and ensemble pieces by noted groups such as the Los Angeles Guitar Quartet.

Tim is also a talented guitarist and singer. He and his daughter Kat Eldred perform together throughout the region. After his years at Interlochen Public Radio, he took year-long classes downstate as a luthier, or one who makes stringed instruments.

I am blessed to have such a skilled artist and friend in life as you, Tim.

TIM BURKE
"PLAYING GUITAR"

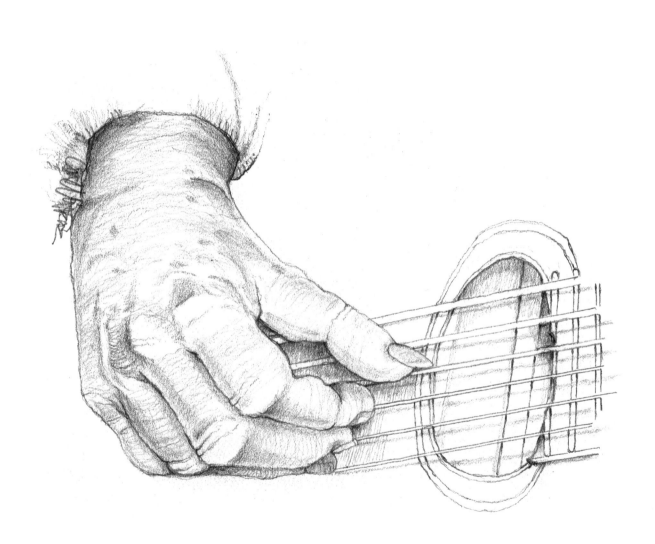

I met Michael Mittelstaedt in a funny chance of circumstances several years ago at the Traverse City Film Festival. My husband Edward was hired, dressed as an old cowboy for the teaser of Michael's first western, "Chasing Daylight".

Michael possesses a bachelor's degree in Spanish Language and Psychology from Michigan State University and a MFA in Film from Ohio University.

He has worked previously as production/director at Broadview Media in Chicago. Michael was also the lead producer for the non-profit For Global Progress, in conjunction with UCLA's Geffen School of Medicine/AIDS Research.

He is an independent filmmaker, educator and director of the Film and New Media program at the internationally renowned Interlochen Center for the Arts in Interlochen, MI.

It has been a pleasure getting to know you Michael, and good fortune with your first Western film.

MICHAEL MITTELSTAEDT
"MOVIE SPOTLIGHT"

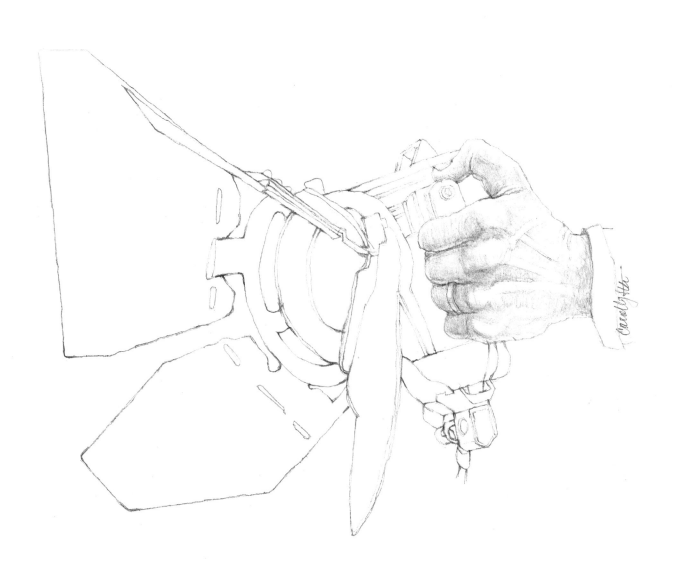

Karl Bielman is a maker, jeweller, graphic artist, history buff, cartoon creator, Star Wars geek, costume designer, scholar and all-round funny guy. He is Artist/Proprietor of his family's unique store, Nawbin Jewelry & Curiosities of Traverse City, MI.

An avid cyclist, bring up the subject of bikes and you shall be enthralled with his stories or description of his collection of bicycles. With his wife and two children, Karl's family is involved in Norte, a bike centric youth advocacy program.

The son of two very artistic and creative parents, Karl is skilled in jewellery making, in addition to assembling pieces of art from a myriad of materials natural or man-made. Nawbin features everything from semi-precious stones, strands of ancient beads, fossils, dinosaur pieces, and global antiquities. Also, of course, Karl's own art projects, plus his jewellry designs made of Michigan stones to exotic treasures.

"If you don't own it, make it", is his mantra.

KARL BIELMAN
"FILING PEWTER"

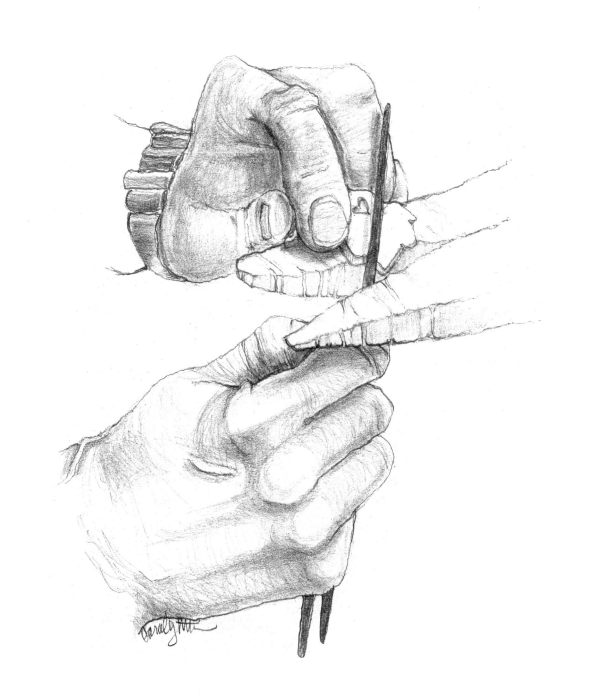

I have known Marty Mack, his parents and extended family almost 30 years. During these years he has been a bike shop mechanic, long distance cyclist, and licensed electrician. But, he is probably best known as a home brewmaster.

"I have been home brewing since I turned 21 in 1998", said Marty. He has always found brewing to be a perfect mix of scientific principles and artistic expression. The best brewer has a good balance between the left and right side of the brain.

In the early days of Facebook, he started a local home brewing group called BREW@HOME. They "met" monthly, simultaneously brewing multiple batches of beer.

Marty has participated in multiple competitions. He won first place in the people's choice and judges' choice the first time he entered the Traverse City Microbrew and Music Festival. He aided the Lake Ann Brewing Company, which opened 2015 in Lake Ann, MI. Marty offered input on the brewing system and helped formulate recipes.

Home brewing is a rewarding hobby that produces delicious beer that is fun to share with friends and family. Home brewing has been a fun part of Marty's life and he is sure he will never completely stop.

Nobody does it better than Marty!

MARTY MACK
"BEER MAKER"

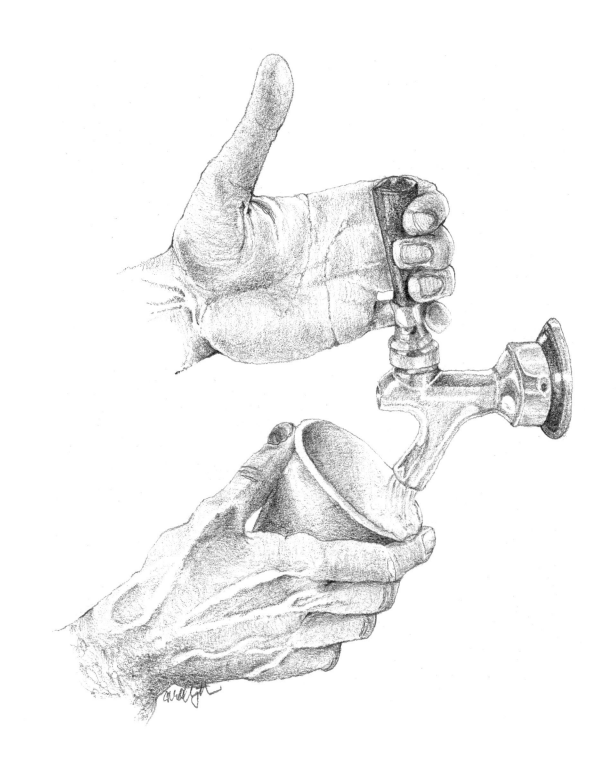

A talented artist, a fellow cyclist, neighbour and man with passion for life, Brian Strickland is a truly multi-faceted man.

I met him years ago at the Candle Factory, housed in the historic gas company building in the Warehouse District downtown. This locale provided the gas for all the city street lights.

His interest of stained glass began in 1965 whilst in junior high. Following college and the US Army, Brian resumed his art. A multiple award winning artist, he has cleverly renovated an old church into his home. The basement is his studio and a colourful, welcoming gallery. Brian's works are thematic, with his bicycle series the most popular.

You create magic with each stained glass piece, Brian. We are honoured with gifts of your artwork. You are among my circle of artistic friends who inspire me.

BRIAN STRICKLAND
"STAINED GLASS"

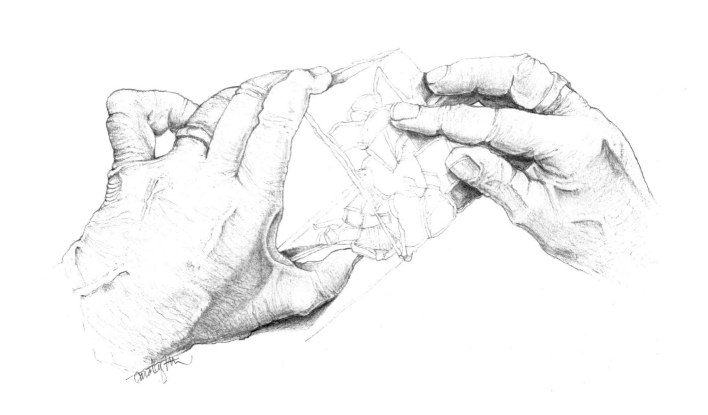

I first met Glenn Wolff in the mid 1980s, he having recently moved home from New York City. He was sharing studio space with photographer John Robert Williams in the heart of downtown Traverse City.

Glenn is an award winning artist, known for his unique style of illustration and paintings. His interpretations of nature are highly recognised. His artwork has been featured in major publications such as *The New York Times, The Village Voice, Audubon, The Central Park Conservancy* as well as in numerous books.

Regionally, he is best known for his illustrations in the natural science books of author Jerry Dennis that include *It's Raining Frogs and Fishes* and *The Bird in the Waterfall*.

He studied printmaking at Northwestern Michigan College in Traverse City, MI, plus has a BFA from the Minneapolis College of Art and Design. He has now come full circle, as a full-time instructor at Northwestern Michigan College.

I also know him as a talented musician who plays the double bass. Glenn owns a beautiful acoustic bass, as well as electric upright. Due to crippling arthritis, I am no longer able to play the bass, knowing the strength it takes to play. I know firsthand the skill and physicality required to play a double bass, and I am reminded of it whenever I listen to Glenn and fellow bassists perform.

I have long admired Glenn in his many artistic talents in the fine arts and music, as an environmentalist, and a soft-spoken gentle man.

GLENN WOLFF
"PLAYING THE BASS"

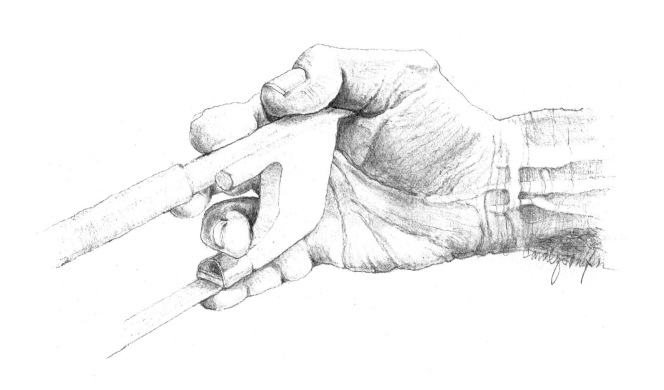

Residing in the culturally diverse region of northern Michigan, I knew Jeff Haas by reputation years before we met. A noted composer and jazz pianist, his unique musical voice is found in the confluence of his lifelong passion for jazz, rhythm and blues, classical and Judaic music.

Raised in a musically rich household, Jeff began his artistic journey seriously studying the classics. When he later asked his father about the Beatles, he was told rock and roll would ruin the needle on the stereo. Soon after, he discovered the 1963 Motown Review, and a clandestine album by Monk and Coltrane's "Live at the Five Spot" hidden in his sister's room.

He went rogue and never looked back.

Jeff founded Building Bridges with the Music program in 1995, performing his original music to K–12 students in over 700 schools throughout Michigan. Drawing from his degree in social work, Jeff and his culturally diverse colleagues share very personal stories about how bullying and prejudice have impacted their lives and engage the students in an open discussion about the importance of open-mindedness and respect.

But it's their music that opens hearts and minds to their message of peace and love.

JEFF HAAS
"PLAYING PIANO"

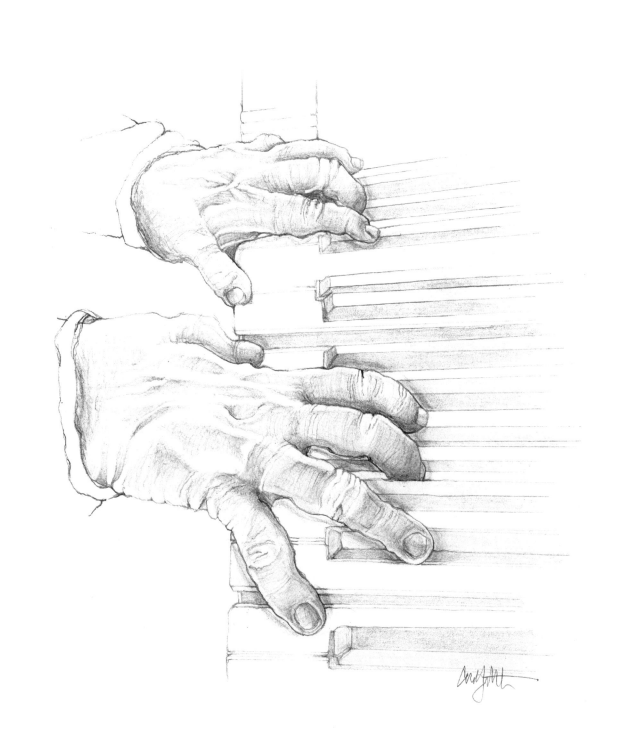

I have known Sue Richards Lee since the first grade. She is an accomplished flutist. We performed with the high school symphony orchestra and Northwest Michigan Symphony Orchestra, known now as the Traverse Symphony Orchestra.

Due to my multiple serious health issues and deformed hands, I no longer have the strength required to play nor ability to carry my favourite musical instrument. I wish I could still perform in ensembles with Sue. Attending concerts and enjoying the music with her is a great substitution.

With a degree in medical technology from Ferris State University in Big Rapids, MI, she applied her skills whilst moving across the country, from Vermont to Montana, and finally New Mexico with her husband Jerry's work. She retired as a research coordinator in OB/GYN at the University of New Mexico. Jerry retired as Indian Prevention Specialist with the Indian Health Services, both of them in Albuquerque.

As newly relocated retirees, they are embarking on the wonders and foibles of an older home, complete with all its demands and repairs.

It is fabulous to have one of my very best friends relocated back home to northwestern Michigan residing just minutes away.

I love you forever, dearest Sue!

SUE RICHARDS LEE
"PLAYING FLUTE"

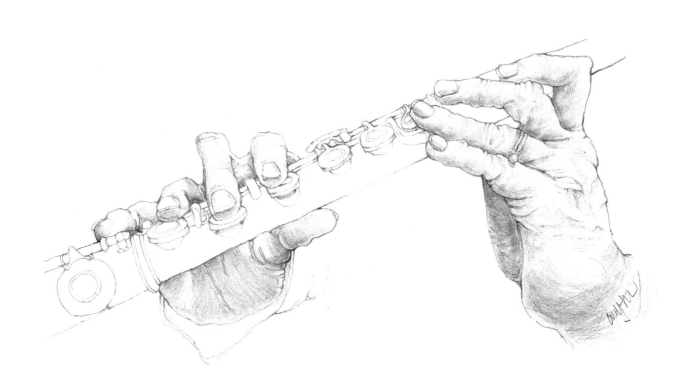

Doug Stanton is a #1 *New York Times* bestselling author. With his wife and fellow writer Anne Gertiser Stanton, plus Grant and Paulette Parsons, Doug created the National Writers Series in 2010. Internationally renowned authors speak before a packed audience, at the historic City Opera House in our city, as they discuss their writing process and anecdotes from their lives.

In 2005, he was one of the co-founders of the highly successful Traverse City Film Festival with John Robert Williams and Michael Moore. He was named a Michiganian of the Year in 2018.

Doug earned a Bachelor of Arts degree majoring in English from Hampshire College in Amherst, Massachusetts. He was also awarded a Masters in Fine Arts from the Writers Workshop at the University of Iowa.

He is recognised for his highly detailed and researched historical books featuring the US military. Doug has received multiple honours and spoken before the US Department of State and the Center for Strategic International Studies.

His award winning books include *In Harm's Way*, a World War II history of the sinking and rescue of the USS Indianapolis; *The Odyssey Of Echo Company* about the Vietnam Tet Offensive; and *Horse Soldiers*, about US Secret Forces embedded in Afghanistan, the first Americans in that region post September 11, 2001. This book became the successful feature film "12 Strong".

It is not every day that one can say they know a New York Times best selling author, a resident of your hometown. I am truly honoured to know you, Doug.

DOUG STANTON
"AUTHOR WRITING"

Cleaning a theatre was William's first job at age 17. As the manager did not work as much as scheduled, William soon became a young assistant manager.

He attended the Berklee College of Music in Boston, MA. Whilst at the college studying music, William was learning at Boston, Light and Sound in proper projector operation by "old school" movie projectionists, the training staff of its union members.

As a member of the Boston Projectionist Union, William explained he was busy as "low man on the totem pole". He became proficient at operating all the projectors at the 15 theatres in the metro area. Boston, Light and Sound maintained all the projection booths throughout the region.

He moved to Traverse City in June 2008, employed as the projectionist at the State Theatre, shortly after the facility opened following major renovation and reopening in 2007. The State has both film and digital format projectors in presenting movies.

William is quite proud he was the projectionist at the State Theatre when it was named the Number One theatre in the world to watch a movie, as awarded by the Motion Picture Association of America.

Ironically, his instructors at Boston, Light and Sound were the same people who designed the State Theatre projection room 25 years after his training by the company.

A man of many talents, his first professional music project earned him a Grammy award. Playing the synthesizer and drums, William performed on Al Green's "Everything's Gonna be Alright", one of the first crossover Gospel/pop tunes.

William is a fascinating man, wise in the ways of the world, a great conversationalist and never boring! You are a fun and enlightening friend.

WILLIAM KESKEY
"THEATRE PROJECTOR"

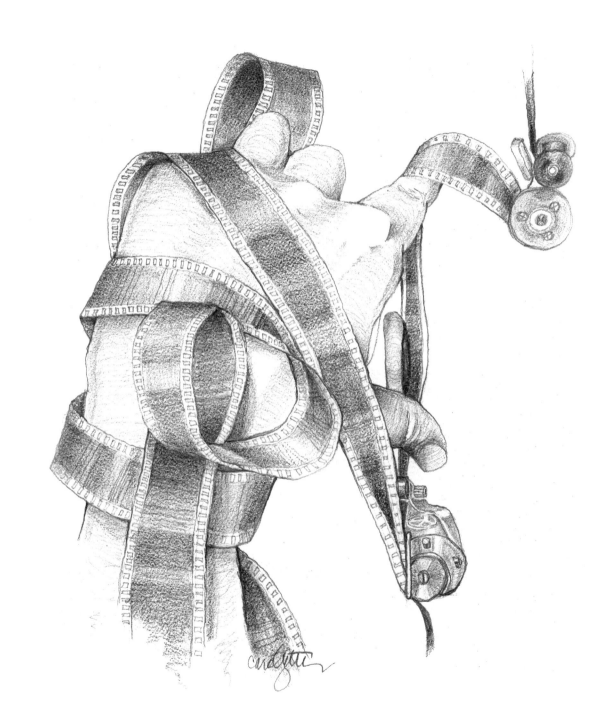

I have the pleasure of knowing Dr. Mark Leslie since high school. A very soft spoken gentle man with a wry sense of humour, he has been putting me back together since the mid-1980s, with surgeries too numerous to mention.

He has medical degrees from Wayne State University, a five year orthopedic surgery residency at Bronson and Borgess Hospitals in Kalamazoo, MI, and a surgery fellowship from Tufts University in Boston, MA. Mark specializes in hand surgery.

In addition to replacing finger joints, repairing broken digits or ruptured ligaments, and fusing my wrists, Mark has also repaired my confidence in my abilities with the many reconstructive surgeries.

He is more than a top rated hand surgeon, he is a very dear friend and someone who I have known and trusted most of my life. I truly would not be here today without him.

Thank you, thank you, Mark!

DR. MARK LESLIE
"EXAMINING HANDS"

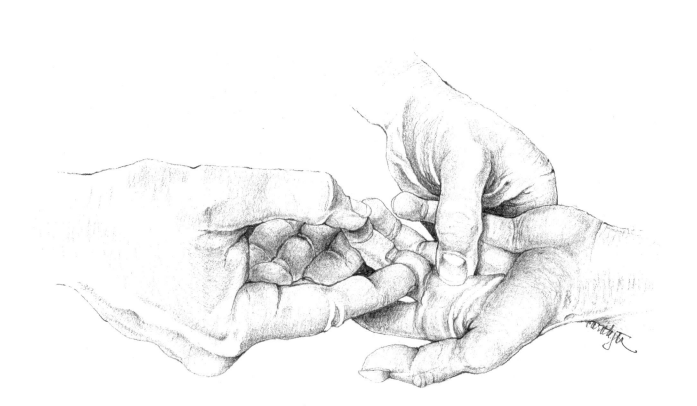

Born and raised in Traverse City, MI, Kim McCloskey and I have known each other for decades, graduating high school together. We reconnected a number of years ago, discovering that she and my husband, Edward, work together as drivers at Bay Area Transportation Authority.

Kim's life has been one filled of journeys. She has travelled and hiked throughout Colorado, as well as exploring the Pacific Crest Trail in Oregon. She has taken the road for adventure of the unknown at all opportunities.

Her greatest journey was as a single parent. Kim is a gorgeous woman with a beautiful heart and soul, as is her daughter.

All of her journeys led her to be a public transportation driver. Kim has been using her hands to steer the wheels on the bus in all kinds of directions.

She is grateful to be living in her hometown, as every day of driving leads to a new adventure in her life and her passengers.

Big hugs and love you, Kim!

KIM McCLOSKEY
"DRIVING AROUND"

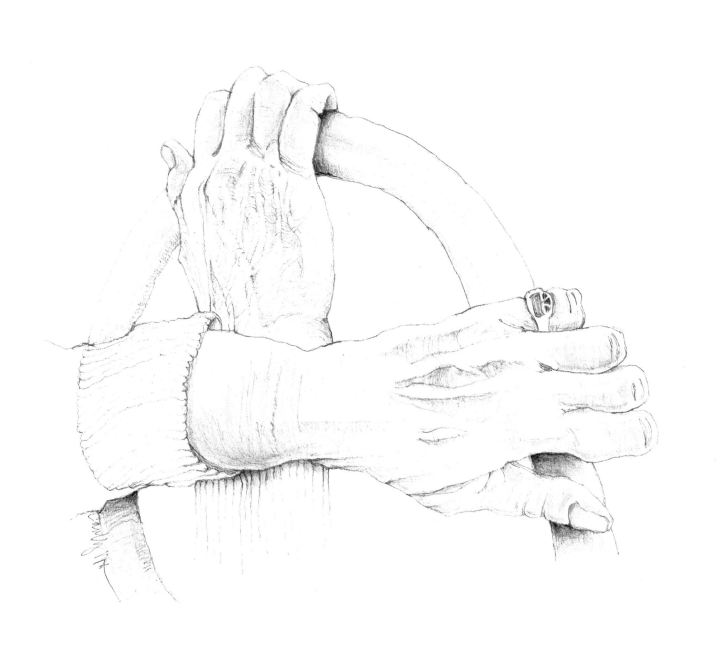

With a perpetual smile, Martha Beard is a humble, kindhearted woman. We have known Marty since the early 1990s, whilst Edward worked at Crystal Mountain Resort near Thompsonville, MI.

She acquired a bachelor's degree in Parks and Recreation from Michigan State University. Her first job after college was teaching skiing at Crystal Mountain. She transitioned to Human Resources, holding that position for 30 years until retiring.

In 2011, Marty and husband Doug purchased Leone's Ice Cream. They are renowned for their specially made ice creams. It's great to see friendly faces doing something they love.

Thank you, Marty!

MARTHA BEARD
"ICE CREAM CONE"

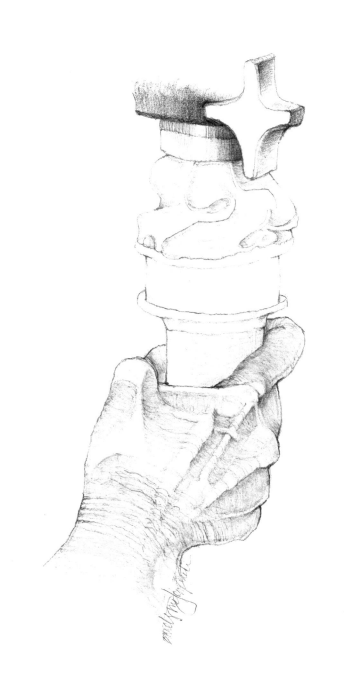

Dr. Flora Biancalana recently retired from her medical practice, the Rising Star Wellness Center located in Traverse City, MI. A holistic practitioner, very down-to-earth woman, my husband and I were patients when she first started her clinic until it's closure many years later.

Edward and myself received excellent care by her and the staff at the clinic, and we truly miss her! She was my favourite doctor and it is a joy whenever our paths cross in town.

Thank you Flora, for years of healing us and countless other people in Northwest Michigan. I hold you in highest esteem as a medical practitioner and person.

A respected physician in our region, I could not consider completing my series without the healing hands of "Doctor B".

DR. FLORA BIANCALANA
"STETHOSCOPE IN HAND"

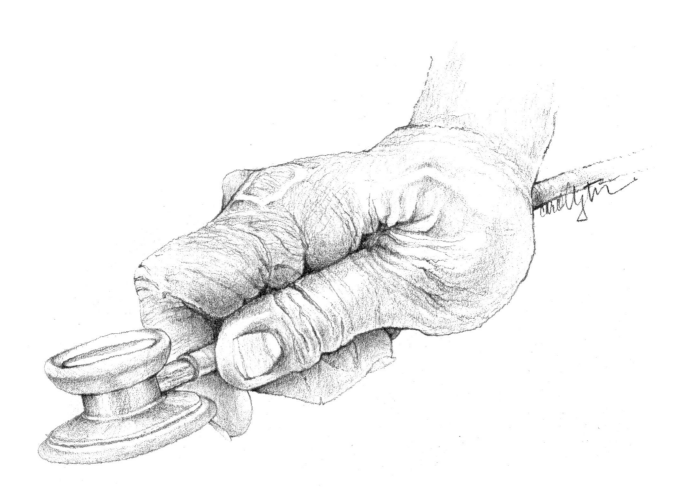

Jim Tuller started his career as a volunteer firefighter. For 30 years, he has been employed with the Traverse City Fire Department, with ten-plus years as Fire Chief.

Being a fire chief is more than directing hot spots to be extinguished at a blaze, community meetings and public events. It involves constant meetings and trainings. The trainings take place locally, downstate and out-of-state. Jim attends numerous fire trainings at the Michigan Firefighter Training Center.

My hero and father, Richard Tompkins, was in the Traverse City Fire Department for 25 years. Growing up, Dad's work was a key part of my childhood days and college years. A fire-related drawing needed to be included, due to the longstanding family connection.

Thank you Chief and neighbour, Jim Tuller.

"Once fire department family, always fire department family!"

FIRE CHIEF JIM TULLER
"ANTIQUE FIRE HELMET"

A leading advocate for women in northwestern Michigan, Marsha Smith has modelled strength and leadership since childhood, beginning in Girl Scouts.

These skills have been an integral part of Marsha's career, primarily in her work with community service and philanthropy. A founding mother of the Women's Resource Center, her work has been directed in empowering women, in many non-profits.

She has been in a myriad of positions of fundraising, including the Women's Resource, Interlochen Center for the Arts and Paul Oliver Hospital.

For twenty-five years, she is best known as the executive director of Rotary Charities, a public foundation that makes grants to non-profit organizations in northwest Michigan. Marsha is most proud of her continual ability to support and open doors for success and opportunity to women.

I am honoured to call Marsha a friend, and a woman I have long admired.

MARSHA SMITH
"OPENING DOORS"

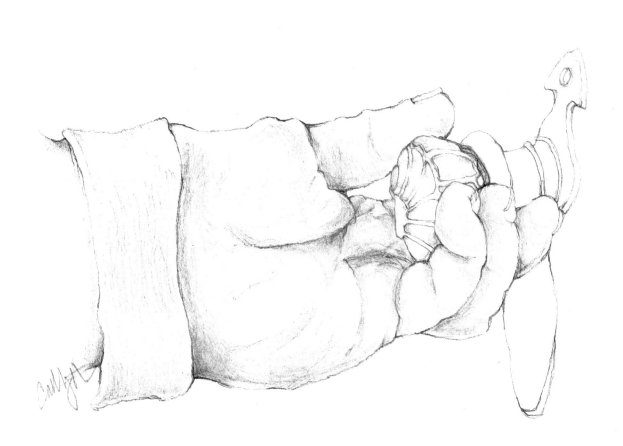

This was one of my first commissioned drawings and I am most proud and honoured it was gifted. Requested by dear friends as a Christmas gift for Nadine Jones, it was drawn using a Xerox of a photo for a reference. It depicts an adult a daughter holding her elderly mother's hand shortly before her death.

Nadine is the recipient of the sensitive hands drawing, holding her mother Pearl Morden's hand. It hangs framed in her local office.

I am doubly honoured as the drawing in notecard form has been used as condolence cards by the Munson Medical Center Infectious Diseases Department in Traverse City, MI.

The bond between a mother and daughter are never broken, no matter the age.

NADINE JONES
"HOLDING ON"

W. Edward Grim, better known as Eddie, is a spiritual man with his beliefs influenced by Native American and Christian teachings. He is equally proud of his Cherokee, Miami and Scottish-Irish heritage. His family has Northern Michigan connections since childhood.

Eddie has Bachelor degrees in sociology and theology from Anderson University, plus a Master in Divinity from Anderson School of Divinity. He was ordained in 1976 and served several pastorates before retiring.

He is past chairman of the American Indian Council, past co-director of the Mik ki si ah wah sis Youth Council and Traverse City LGBTQ community.

I do not know anyone with a more diverse spirituality, commitment to community and advocate for justice than Eddie. I am blessed to call him my friend.

EDDIE GRIM
"HOLY COMMUNION"

I met the delightful Rita Hansen at an annual Christmas Day open house, hosted by my dear friends Chris Bazzett and her husband Ben Hansen.

Using a reference photo, Ben and Chris commissioned me to draw Rita and Bernard Hansen's hands on their wedding day in 1954, as a gift to Rita.

I have long admired the quiet grace and faith of Rita and am privileged to call her a friend, or occasionally "Mom".

RITA HANSEN
"WEDDING HANDS"

I have known John Robert Williams for most of my life. He, his wife Terrie Taylor, who I have known since kindergarten, and myself graduated high school together in Traverse City, MI.

He was "bit" by the photography bug in 1975 whilst taking classes with noted photographer Steve Ballance at Northwestern Michigan College in Traverse City. He continued his studies at the William James College of Grand Valley State University in Grand Rapids, MI. One of his mentors was Bob Burns, father of documentary filmmaker Ken Burns.

Whilst in Grand Rapids, John started a multi-media business, which he brought back to his hometown. He had his studio in the heart of downtown Traverse City for decades until relocating into an immense work space.

Civic minded, he has served on numerous boards including the Rotary Club of Traverse City, Rotary Charities and Rotary Camps and Services. John helped form the Affordable Housing Task Force, the Traverse Area Recreation Trail (TART), is co-founder of the Traverse City Film Festival, and assisted in the renovation of the State Theatre, which is run by the film festival.

John and his brother David are renowned for secretly entering the Cherry Royale Parade of the National Cherry Festival. For 22 years, they spoofed royalty with floats, props and willing, unsuspecting participants. A small band of us dedicated, merry workers annually contributed to the surprise Williams Brothers' parade entry.

An avid photographer and cyclist, John is passionate making Traverse City a better place to live, work and grow.

This book would not exist without the photographic and computer talents of my dear friend. I lack the words to sufficiently thank you for everything you have done bringing my dream to fruition.

Thank you, John!

JOHN ROBERT WILLIAMS
"PHOTOGRAPHER"

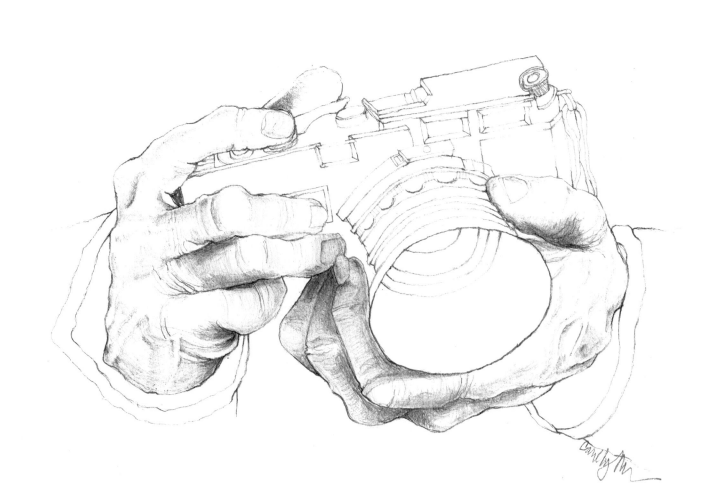

Acknowledgements

This book would not be possible without the following people:

Edward Parker, my husband who has always believed in me;

John Robert Williams, a very dear friend who graciously provided his services as photographer for my book and to whom I am eternally indebted;

Anne Gertiser Stanton, editorial director at Mission Point Press, Traverse City, MI, who said "we need to make a book of your unique drawings";

Heather Shaw, design and production director, also of Mission Point Press;

Marketing Director Tricia Frey and computer guru Hart Cauchy, both of Mission Point Press;

Doug Weaver, business manager, and another guiding light from Mission Point Press;

The Botanic Garden at the Historic Barns, for giving me permission to draw under the giant pavilion overlooking Traverse City;

Grace Episcopal Church, for allowing me to draw in a basement classroom secluded and free from distractions; and

To every person who participated and allowed me to draw their hands —

Thank you — and cheers!

CPSIA information can be obtained
at www.ICGtesting.com
Printed in the USA
LVHW071725300321
682966LV00002B/19